Here
and
Beyond

Here
and
Beyond

By
Raymond Bottomley

authorHOUSE®

AuthorHouse™
1663 Liberty Drive
Bloomington, IN 47403
www.authorhouse.com
Phone: 1-800-839-8640

Published by AuthorHouse   02/27/2012

ISBN: 978-1-4678-9006-9 (sc)
ISBN: 978-1-4678-9007-6 (e)

Contents

Part Two
Be a Better Person

Prologue

I have always had dozens of questions about life: Where do we come from? Why are we here? What happens to us when we die?

Do you, like me, continually question everything? Are you seeking reason and truth? This book won't be able to answer all of your questions, but at the very least it will open up your mind to what life is really all about—and awaken you to your own potential.

In order to understand the contents of this book, it is important for you first to open your mind to every possibility. Don't allow yourself to be blinded by your parents' beliefs or those indoctrinated into you throughout your life. And be prepared to invest some emotion in the search. If your outlook is passionless, then you won't be able to enjoy life's beautiful truth to the full.

So forget everything you believe regarding religion and faith and start with a blank canvas, a freshly rubbed-out blackboard. Have a brand new stick of chalk in your hand ready to write a new life and a completely fresh set of beliefs, rules or guidelines, whatever you want to call them. Be willing to open up your mind and your spirit to the truth.

In the first part of this book I detail the various aspects of the truth as I see it. In the second part I give some suggestions for helping you to lead a better life and improve yourself.

Ask yourself one simple question: Am I ready for my life to be changed? Once you do open your eyes fully to the truth your life will be truly changed, and for the better.

And once you know the truth, don't disregard it in your daily life. Make sure that you use it for the greater good by helping others. It only takes a minute of your time to offer someone help, but it may lead to hours of unhappiness for them if you don't.

Once you have finished the last word on the last page, please go ahead and help somebody with the new and exciting knowledge you have learned. Pass it on!

Part One

The Glorious Truth

White Light

Where shall we begin on our journey together? The best place to start is at the beginning.

Empty your mind for a moment, forget your day-to-day worries, breathe deeply and prepare yourself for enlightenment.

In the beginning

In the beginning there was light . . .

That is how the bible begins. I haven't read the bible in its entirety, but I do know that it contains many wonderful parables about life and offers a sound and sensible guide to how to live.

While most people do not take the bible literally—Darwin's theory of evolution and the science of the big bang have disproved the concept of God making the world in six days and creating Eve from Adam's rib, for example—many do recognise and accept its spiritual content. The bible is the world's oldest and bestselling book and it has changed the lives of many people.

Maybe the bible is so popular because it offers hope; or maybe it is there to be challenged, so that in doing so we can establish the truth.

In my view, there are two fundamental things that we should extract from the bible and hold close to our hearts: the parables—simple tales about normal people and the positive attributes they offer to others—and the story of Jesus of Nazareth.

I do believe the story of Jesus. In my opinion he is the most important character in the bible. We should read about, remember and learn from Jesus—not because of Christianity, but because of who he was and still is, and what he represents.

Jesus is the head of government of the world of the spirit. He is our Lord and hopefully one day our saviour.

The infinite light

So in the beginning there was light. There was a bright white light that was and is the source of all life. That bright white light is the source of the energy from which everything comes and to which we return when our time on this earth ends.

It is an infinite light that has always been there and will always be there—no beginning and no end.

It is the life force of everything, giving everything a purpose—love, learning and personal progression towards pure love and perfection.

Our universe is much larger than we think. It is both simple and complex at the same time, and the true facts about it are beyond human thought and comprehension. There are millions of universes, all needing each other to maintain balance for the structure of existence. There are dark holes, there is the fabric of space, there is nothingness and there is also the opposite, positive energy. All these energies work together in perfection and balance.

If all of the aspects of space are limitless and infinite, and if we are born from these energies, then this is proof enough that we—as people, as spirits or souls—are also limitless and infinite. We are singular, but we are also collective, because we are all part of the same energy.

If you were to take a football stadium and fill it full of peas, the football stadium would represent our sun and one pea would represent the earth. That's how big our sun is compared to the earth. Can you imagine that?

However, there are other suns that can be represented by the football stadium and then our sun would be like a pea within it. Can you imagine that?

You are a better person than me if you can understand the full magnitude of this. It is beyond our imagination.

The ability to acknowledge and understand fully the magnitude of life has deluded the human race for eons. It is like the white light—we cannot see it and we also cannot understand it, but it is there.

The white light is eternal, it is energy, it is the building block of all things spiritual. It has no beginning and it has no end—and neither do we.

Once you allow your mind to digest and accept this, it starts to open up many other opportunities. Don't question it, just accept it.

Simple and complex

We don't need to question the white light simply because our mind cannot grasp its technical achievement or comprehend its simplicity.

This simplicity consists in the fact that the white light exists and has done for ever, and will continue on for ever. It is a little like numbers and money. We know what one pound is, we can even get to grips with one million pounds as you can win that on a TV show, but there is a line where our mind cannot stretch any further. We can't get our head round numbers such as a billion or a trillion pounds. It is similar with the white light and the existence of life.

The white light *is* life.

You may be saying to yourself that life is you sitting there reading this book, breathing in the air, scratching your nose. Of course you are right, in relation to the life we live at present here on earth. But there are millions and millions of planets, in fact an infinite number of planets in an infinite number of solar systems. We are only one small part of life and one very small part of existence.

Is the white light heaven? Yes and no. The white light is everything and all spiritual matter is white light. The white light is the spirit world, and the spirit world comes from the white light.

We are spirit and we are white light. All solid, earthly matter is carbon and water based, and all spiritual matter is white light—spiritual energy. The Chinese call it 'chi', the Japanese 'ki'. To new age travellers it is better known as cosmic energy, and Native Americans call it 'Prana' or the Great White Spirit.

Chi

Chi is the Chinese name for the white light. It is the natural energy of the universe, which permeates everything. All matter, from the smallest atoms and molecules to the largest planets and stars, is made up of this energy. It is the vital force of life. It is the source of every existing thing.

Chi is the power that enables us to think, move, breathe and live—the power that makes gravity act like gravity. It is what makes electricity electric. It is our connection to the flow of the universe and the prime moving force within the human body.

Chi is not breath; it is the power that makes it possible for us to breathe. Chi is not simply 'energy', it is what gives energy the power to be energy. Chi is in the oxygen we breathe and the blood that flows through us.

Chi cannot be seen or measured, it cannot be touched or captured. It is everywhere, yet we have no way to make it tangible or even prove its existence. Therefore Chi is a difficult concept to accept.

Chi within the body is like power in a rechargeable battery. Occasionally it needs to be replenished. The Chi of the universe is inexhaustible, yet the body needs fresh Chi to maintain its vitality. When you are exchanging the Chi within you with the Chi of the universe, you feel healthy and vigorous, able to fight off illness and maintain good health.

The power of Chi

Try an experiment on yourself and see how you can tap into Chi and use it to have an instant physical effect.

Look at the palms of your hands—both hands at the same time. Each hand has line and marks, but also each wrist has a horizontal line. Hold your hands together so that the sides touch and the lines of your hands meet up. Once you have lined up the marks, close your hands together like in prayer. You will find that the fingers on one hand will be shorter than the other.

Do the same again. Line up the markings on your hands but, before clasping your hands into the prayer position, close your eyes and ask the universe to make your shorter fingers longer. Breathe in and out through your nose and ask calmly in your mind for the universe to shower you with the positive energies of Chi and make your shorter fingers longer.

Open your eyes and clasp your hands together like in prayer. You may have felt a tingling in your fingers before you placed your hands together. Your shorter fingers will be longer, as you asked.

You have just scratched the surface of Chi and the wonderment of its power.

The Great White Spirit

Like Chi, the Great White Spirit is the life energy of everything.

Human beings, as personalities, are spirit. We come from the Great White Spirit and we go back to it when our body ceases to exist. We do not die, but the miracle of existence that is the human body does.

Take time to investigate the human body. By doing so you will understand and appreciate more of what a miracle your body actually is.

The human body has been designed to enable us to live on this planet. It works in harmony with the earth's gravitational pull, it battles with its antibodies through some ingenious self-protection called the immune system, and it breathes in the earth's oxygen, manufactured by its own set of lungs—trees.

We breathe in oxygen and breathe out carbon dioxide. The earth's trees breathe in carbon dioxide through a process called photosynthesis and thus exhale oxygen. This is humanity working and living in harmony with the earth, our own life support system.

The good and the bad

But if the Great White Spirit is that clever, that good, then why aren't we living better lives, without crime or evil or pain and suffering? If the powers of the universe are that great, then is the spirit playing games with us? Is it cruel?

All bad things are done by us—the human race—not the great white spirit. Most of us are inherently good, but individually we all make mistakes. We talk about people behind their backs, judge others, are selfish and greedy, squander and waste resources.

The earth is a living organism, a life form that makes life and sustains life. All animals on this earthly plane come from spirit, and return to spirit when they die. All animals are here through the miracle of evolution and are here for a purpose.

All life forms live in complete harmony with the earth. They live in the trees, the ground and the air. They feed from the earth and what the earth produces.

The earth is a gift for us to enjoy, respect and love, but what do we do? We destroy the environment, we rape the world of its natural resources, we hunt and kill beautiful animals for fun and financial gain.

We as human beings live in small boxes, isolated from the earth. Whereas animals work with the earth, we rape and pillage its natural resources. We pump millions of cubic metres of carbon dioxide into the atmosphere, eroding the protection barrier from the sun's rays. The ice sheets are melting, the sea levels are rising and we are seeing more and more flooding.

The equilibrium of the earth is changing and seasons, instead of being clear and defined, are blending into one. This alone sends confusing information to the animal kingdom, which exists on structure and format.

But if you look at the earth, really look at it without pessimistic glasses on, then you will see something of beauty and wonder. Miracles happen every day: rain, clouds, storms, grass, mountains, the ocean. Our world spins on its axis so fast that it looks as though it is not even moving.

Open your eyes. Look at the trees, look at the animals, look up on a clear night and look at all of the stars and appreciate the wonder—appreciate all of the miracles.

Stop taking life for granted and understand its miracles. Start watching some nature programmes, read more about the earth and yourself as a human being. Take in as much information as you can.

There is no evil, no crime, no greed in the light—we know what we need to learn, to experience, in order to become a better person, and we chose to come back here to live this life in order to experience life's lessons. You may have been cruel in a previous life and have to rectify this. Or you may have had wealth and life's riches and need to experience poverty.

You need to experience the dark to appreciate the light.

We are here to learn

We are here not because of the Great White Spirit, but because we *asked* to be. And we are here for a reason: to learn, to improve ourselves and to help one another.

Stop reading, take a breath and look around you. Look out of window and see the trees, the wind if there is any, and the rain if it is raining. Go outside and feel the warmth of the sun on your skin. You're smiling, aren't you? Once you remember to appreciate the earth, life starts to soften a little.

The earth belongs to us and it has been made for us to live here throughout our life—to sustain us and bring us joy. But it has also been designed as somewhere for us to live while we learn to be better. The spirit world is much higher in the ranks than the earth. We have to be here to experience the bad, so that we appreciate the better all the more.

If you want to learn how to ride a horse, you don't go to the supermarket, you go to a riding school. If you want to learn how to drive a car, you don't do it online or via a computer game, you go to a driving instructor.

Similarly, there are lessons that can only be learnt by living in the physical world, where the tests of our spirit can be experienced. You can't learn them in the spirit world, as they are conditions that simply do not exist. Here on earth, we can experience primitive but important situations that build and strengthen us as spiritual energies.

In addition, you can't really help someone who is suffering unless you have suffered yourself. You can be a shoulder to lean on, but you will not truly appreciate their suffering unless you can empathise—empathy is born though shared experiences.

Appreciate the wonder of the world and your experience. If you have a pet, give it a cuddle and say thank-you for the friendship your pet gives you. Look at your family and thank them for the love and support you have for each other.

Change one thing

Now you have all of these good thoughts in your head, ask yourself one question: If I could change one thing about me, what would that be? I don't mean appearance or weight or clothes, I mean you as a person—what would you change about you?

Your spirit is the part of you that is asking the questions. We are all in need of improvement—becoming friendlier towards strangers, giving to people in need, smiling more or giving more time to our family, being able to build bridges with our siblings, being better to our boss and so on.

We all need to grow and become better. That is why we are here.

Each of us is in fact two people, two beings—spirit energy and a human body, both linked as one. The spiritual body stems from a higher level of life but is allowed to exist on a lower level, human existence. We are here to learn how to become better, and the only way to learn is to allow our higher level of consciousness to prevail and to be nicer, more loving, more appreciative, more giving.

If you are a builder or a joiner, for example, you learn through experience. If you were to ask a builder or plumber whether he had learnt all was there to learn about his trade, he would say no and confirm that he was learning something new every day.

The same applies to all of us. We continually need to learn, striving for perfection—and we have infinity during which to improve.

The five truths

We do not need to question how we are living and where, we need to understand and accept the truth.

To sum up, the five main truths are:

1. We are from a higher level of existence.
2. We have been given our human body and the earth as a gift.
3. We are here to learn as part of our spiritual growth.
4. We live eternally.
5. We have chosen to be here.

We will look at these in more depth in the following chapters.

Birth

As a spiritual being we will never die, as we constitute an eternal energy and come from the Great White Spirit, which is life itself. At the same time, our body is the vehicle that enables us to exist on planet earth, and for that there has to be a start. There has to be a spark to generate life.

Through the miracle of childbirth, we are born as near-blind, helpless beings who need 24-hour care from our parents. We feed on milk until our stomach develops to the point where it can digest solid food and rid itself of the waste product.

We begin to see, sense and hear everything at a very early age, but our brain is not developed enough to store and react to the information it is processing.

Soon we can interact and bond with our mother and share love throughout our life, from being a baby to starting school; heading towards puberty and thinking about sex and peer pressure and style; getting a job and learning to stand on our own two feet; then completing that wonderful circle of life where we become parents ourselves.

All of these exciting miracles of change happen in a relatively short period of time—time that seems endless when we are young, but very short as we get older.

The process of life itself is infinite, and we all have a family tree of ancestors going back to a point in time that we fail to comprehend, thousands of people linked to us by family bonds and genetic connections.

Birth as a spiritual being

So we start our life at some point and we know how we are made and born as a human, but how are we made and born as a spiritual being?

I'm a big believer in the saying: 'If it ain't broke, don't fix it.' So to my mind the format for physical birth has been developed and based on that for spiritual birth. Imagine the simplicity of that.

Two spiritual beings, in love, sharing their lives together. What is the most blessed thing all married couples wish for? A family, surely.

As soon as you are born in spirit, I believe that you come here, to the earth. That is the condition that the spiritual parents are aware of when they decide to have a spirit child. As soon as the energy for a spiritual being is formed from two other energies, then that spark of life enters a human body and the human mother is pregnant—at that second in time, the energy passes from the spirit world into the mother's womb.

The child will progress in life, with the single goal of sustaining the Holy Spirit and generating and sharing love. The spiritual parents will be able to watch over the child, see it grow and be there to help in its spiritual progression through thought.

Imagine the emotional wrench for the spiritual parents. Some spiritual mothers may feel that the distress of saying goodbye to their child is too much to bear, and that they need to be part of the child's life in some form.

The spiritual parents may decide that they want a more 'hands-on' approach to the upbringing of their new child. So they may want to come back to earth to share every emotion and every moment with their new baby.

How would that be possible?

Reincarnation

At some time down the line of time, if we choose to, we can start life on earth all over again under a new identity: a new life with new parents, new friends and new beginnings.

If we want, we can discuss, develop and make plans to come back as a family unit. We can decide with our loved ones who will be who during this journey back to earth, so that we can try to relearn things that we should have before, correct wrongs, or just help somebody else with their return, as a player in the whole scheme of things. We can return to be with our new baby.

The idea of reincarnation, and the thought of once having lived here before, possibly as several different people, used to be a difficult concept for me.

Assuming that it is for you too, I am going to repeat for you the questions I asked myself, and the answers I reached over time through meditation.

1. If life is infinite and I've been here before, maybe several times, where are these other people now? I know that their bodies are dead, but where are they as individuals, as spiritual energies?
2. After I die and pass over to the light, if I want to come back as somebody else I then have no knowledge of 'me', only the person that's here on earth now. Where

is the 'me' that I was and what am I doing during the life of this new person?

3. Why come back as somebody else and not 'me'?
4. Why do we have no knowledge of our previous lives?

To start to give you the answers, I should explain that I went to see a psychic development teacher some time ago, and without regression he told me who I was in my previous lives. He stated that I was a monk, a knight of the realm and a North American Indian called Black Eagle. He then said to me that he felt I would have made a good policeman, which in fact I had thought about at one point in this life. He explained that part of my spiritual growth as a knight of the realm was as a kind of policeman, and that is where I got the calling. He also said that I was a martial arts master, which was interesting as I have always had a hidden interest in the martial arts. Finally, being a North American Indian is definitely where I get my interest in spiritual matters. All of this seemed very credible and I did not have any difficulty in believing it.

What was interesting was that even after having been given this privileged information, you might have thought that I would have spent all my time finding out about me and who I was previously. I didn't. I did Google Black Eagle but couldn't find anything out, and I didn't investigate the knight or the monk. Why? I already knew who they were—they were me!

It's like having previous jobs. Once I was a knight, once a monk and once a Native American, and now I am just me. So where are all the memories?

Memories

I have all of the memories right here; I just do not know how to tap into them. They are in my spiritual mind, my subconscious—what you might call my hard drive.

We have plenty to deal with here on earth without having our mind blown by all the things we have done previously. The information is there, for us to use when we need to.

Do you have all of your memories of being a child? Of course not. So if you can't remember aspects of your current life, is it so surprising that you are unable to remember aspects of a previous life?

Furthermore, our brain has not been programmed with these physical memories because it has not lived the memories, whereas our spiritual mind has. Every second of every day of every year is stored in our spiritual mind. We would be in information overload if we remembered everything. And too many memories would hinder our ability to grow in this visit to earth. That is why all of these memories are not readily available for us to think about—or worry about.

No time

When I die, return to the spirit world and then come back, where is the previous me? My new body has no memories of me and I have no recall of my new life. So where am I for 70 years or so? Am I asleep?

The physical body only lives on this planet for an average of three score years and ten. That is why you cannot come back as *you*, because physically you have expired, but at the same time as a spiritual being you are alive and well and feeling the best you have ever felt. In order to understand what happens when you are reincarnated (if you want to be), we need to think about *time*.

Time is a manmade concept in order to measure the seasons and the individual sections of those seasons—seconds, days, weeks, months. Time is a physical thing, not a spiritual one, and therefore there is no measure of time in the spirit world. A year on earth can be a heartbeat in the spirit world.

As humans our lives are controlled by time. Clocks and watches tell us what time to start work, when to pick up our children from school, when to catch the flight for our holiday and so on. We are so brainwashed by time that we cannot understand or even accept a life without it.

But there is no need for time in the spirit world as there are no nights, no days, just one level of existence, a level of existence that is perfect.

Instant sleep

Another way of explaining why we don't have memories of previous lives is that we sleep for hours each night and awaken without any memories.

Have you ever experienced instant sleep, when you are so tired that you fall asleep as soon as your head hits the pillow? You sleep so deeply, probably for eight or nine hours, but you awake as though it was a moment ago. That is instant sleep.

What is stopping us having a spiritual instant sleep, only to awaken and have the memories of another lifetime in what seems like a moment?

It is clear that the concept of reincarnation is both very complex and also very simple.

The Summer Lands

Some people call the spirit world the summer lands, as the summer is the favourite earthly season. Warm sunshine, not too hot, a light cool breeze, and beautiful blue skies with the odd fluffy cloud.

This is our home—our true home. It is where we come from, it is where we are born and it is where we go back to when our physical bodies cease to exist. It is where all of the loved ones we have lost live and look over us every day.

When we pass over we know we are going home. Many stories have been told of people having near death experiences and talking of feeling calm and going home, not wanting to come back.

I read a book once about a pastor who had died many years ago and told his story through a medium, who in turn wrote the book.

The pastor told of his memories when he died. He had been suffering from a long-term illness many years before when medicine was still in its infancy, and reported how suddenly, out of nowhere, he was looking down at himself lying in bed. There was no pain or suffering. In a moment he was travelling at great speed into a bright white light, but he felt no fear, only an excited expectation.

He was greeted by two people whom he did not know, who introduced themselves with smiles and open arms. They had decided that when they passed over it was this job they both wanted to do, as seeing the expressions of those arriving home gave them the most joy.

What hit me when I read the book was the pastor's appearance. He saw a reflection of himself and he was wearing a coat. When he asked his new friends what it was, they said it was his spiritual coat, a coat of energy and colours that reflected him as a person so that strangers could read who he was. In time, as he spiritually progressed in the spirit world, he could relinquish the coat, he could wear what clothes he wanted or just see himself as pure energy. All of these things would become clearer to him in time.

In the book he also commented on his general appearance. He looked like a younger man and was told that he would reflect the time in his life when he felt the best, physically, mentally and spiritually. It was this best time that had lodged itself within his subconscious and it was this phase of his life that had been prepared for his passing. Prepared for him, by him.

He was told that he was in the summer lands, a beautiful place made for people like him when they first pass over. A place that would make him feel calm and at peace and at home with like-minded people.

Our true home

I believe that the summer lands are our real home, where our relatives and friends live after passing over. I also believe that, once you pass over and experience the truth, the first thing you want to do is tell those on earth about this wonderful place, to put their minds at rest and confirm that life is wonderful and everlasting.

There is order and hierarchy in the spirit world and the infinite spiritual realms, as on earth.

When we are children, we progress through the years at school, each year offering a higher level of education. Then we possibly go to university or college or get a job. As the years go by we are still learning constantly. The more we learn the more opportunities arise, either offering a better standard of life and/or further education.

It is this process that is in existence in the spiritual realms.

There are opportunities to learn, to improve and to progress to higher realms. You can stay in the summer lands if you like; it is your choice. But I am sure that when the truth is offered to you the majority of people will jump at the chance of spiritual progression and aiming towards that impossible goal called perfection.

I would also like you to consider that there are an infinite number of summer lands. Let's consider a man called Abdul. Throughout his life he has believed in Islam, to the point that, in his mind, all other individuals are infidels if they are not followers of his faith.

We are all free to believe what we want. However, there is only one truth. All religions have only two things in common: a belief in a higher existence; and love.

When Abdul dies and passes over, he will still be a staunch believer in Islam. Why should he go somewhere he will not be happy? He will pass over to a world with other Muslims who believe the same, so that he can reside with like-minded people. He will be happy and content with his new life. However, if he chooses, he will be offered the opportunity to explore alternative ways of thinking, with the view of considering the one truth, which is the Spirit.

Any regrets?

The summer lands offer the best physical existence we could experience. We can choose where we live. We can be reunited with our loved ones and make new friends. We can enjoy the drink and food that we loved so much here on earth, but will not need them. We sleep here on earth to recharge our batteries, and that still applies when we pass over. We need rest to recharge our spiritual energy.

Your first few times in the summer lands will not be too much different from living on earth. The changes, if you want them, will only occur when you are ready for them.

You will realise how wonderful physical life really is, and you will probably have regrets: that you have smoked, or drank too much, or didn't look after your body the way you should. It is then that you will start to analyse yourself and what you did or did not achieve.

If you have any regrets, your first time in the summer lands will be the point at which they will occur. You will start to judge yourself because you will recognise why you were on the earth in the first place. You chose to live on earth because you had things to do, to put right. You had things to learn. The problem is, you realise that you didn't. You got caught up with the things that physical people want and need, and maybe made some bad decisions along the way.

There is no one judging you except yourself. You are the one who decided that you would go on this journey to earth and it will be you who judges the level of success you have achieved during your journey. It is then that you can decide on your soul plan.

Your Soul Plan

At the beginning of this book, I asked you to open up your mind to accept all possibilities. This is one of the times when you need to open your mind a little further.

I want you to imagine that you are living in the spirit world. You are with your loved ones who passed over before you, and now you know the beautiful truth about life and the extraordinary things that come with it.

You know that this is your real home, and that your stay on earth was short in comparison to the scheme of things. You also know that your stay on earth was a planned journey.

You no longer need cigarettes, alcohol or drugs. You no longer need to eat large amounts of food, or stick your fingers down your throat after a meal to avoid getting fat. You no longer hate yourself when you look at a reflection because you think you are fat or ugly.

Nobody will judge you, ridicule you or taunt you ever again—they will just be courteous and want to help. They will simply smile because they know the truth and relish it.

You no longer need money and the spite and greed that come with it. You know that you can live in a house you like and no longer need to worry about the cost.

You no longer feel any pain, anguish, fear or hate. You just feel love, and relief that you will never die and that everything is available to you.

Furthermore, you know that there are millions of people living on earth who would dearly love to know what you know now, and you also know that one day they will. You have the sacred information that is the Holy Grail everybody has been looking for, for thousands of years. And you may want to do something very important with this information in time, or you may not.

If you did, what could you do?

Change just one person's life

Spiritual progression is a rite and also a choice. The only person you can really help is yourself, through progression.

Don't get me wrong: life back home in the summer lands is glorious and fantastic. But nothing is ever perfect, as perfection is unattainable. You can only strive towards perfection and become the best person you can.

When I pass over, I would love to be a star, a personality. In the spirit world a totally unknown person on earth can be a celebrity.

In the UK there was a woman who was terminally ill with cancer. She did not curl up and die, full of regret, despair and hate; far from it. She spent the remaining years of her life raising an extraordinary amount of money for charities, which in turn gave help to hundreds of people. She was serene, she never complained and she always smiled. I am sure there were tough times and pain, but to those who saw her on television, she was special. To my mind she will be a celebrity in the spirit world—an angel.

If you change just one person's life for the better while living your short time on earth, then your whole life here was worthwhile.

You also have the chance to make somebody's life better on earth while living in the spirit world. You can become a guide and help one person or several people by guiding them through positive thought. This will take time, as you will have to learn how to be a guide. Even though the opportunity is there, you will still need to learn how to do it.

You don't need money, so the job you decide on will be out of choice, not necessity. And if that job means that you have to learn a physical lesson, then so be it.

You may suffer from insecurity, and to help you combat that you may need, as part of your learning, to visit the physical plane once more. If you do, you will have to plan a revisit or reincarnation. Again, this is something you just cannot do, you will need help.

You may buy a new car here on earth. You can drive it, but you may have no idea how fix it if it breaks down. When that happens you may have to employ the services of a mechanic. This also applies to the spirit world—a trained reincarnation engineer, let's say.

Friends and family

Other people may, for various reasons, want to be involved in your reincarnation. They may be friends or relatives in the spirit world or complete strangers. But after a time—it may seem like years—you decide that you want to come back and you have a team of people who will be part of this. One may be your birth mother, a partner or just a friend. They may have lessons that they need to learn, or things to put right, and coming on this journey with you would be ideal for them.

A few years ago, I watched a television programme about a young boy in Mexico, 9 or 10 years old. He had told his mother that he was actually her father in a previous life. He told her things that only her father would know. Amazing, isn't it? She was totally oblivious to the soul plan they had made, and the boy would also have had no idea of the arrangement, but his subconscious channels were open and his conscious mind was able to recollect the memories.

What you have to understand is that all aspects of your immediate family for your new life on earth have to be part of the soul plan. You make an agreement. And by the time this agreement has been put into place and the 'go' button has been pressed, 5, 30, 80 or even hundreds of earth years could have elapsed. There are no restrictions.

If you are here now, you are either a new spirit or you are reincarnated. It is only when you die and pass over to the spirit world, and you debrief yourself, that the lives and lessons you have learnt unwind for you to see. All of this is done to improve you as a person—the kind of self-improvement I address in Part Two.

If you knew about all these lives and lessons while you were living on earth, all of the information would be mind blowing, but it would also cloud the real reason you are here in the first place. You have to learn without any hindrance and be free of interfering thoughts.

For now, just remember that you planned to be here—and you planned your soul plan.

Pain and Suffering

So you planned to be here as part of your soul plan, and you also planned your life and the fixed statuses that form its structure. Pain and suffering are either self-imposed or imposed on you.

Let's consider this in more detail.

You selected your parents and your parents selected you. You were totally aware of the physical ailments that your parents would have, and in turn possibly pass on to you genetically.

Take me as an example. My father has high blood pressure and a stroke ended his life. My mother had a heart problem, and when she died she could not breathe and she eventually died of heart failure. When I spoke to her sister, she remarked how uncanny it was watching her suffer, as she had exactly the same symptoms and ailments as their mother, and both died at the same time in their lives.

Remember that there are always three to four generations living on earth at any one time: you, your parents and your grandparents, and even your great-grandparents. All of these generations have planned their soul plan and thus their reincarnations together. Once again, this is so simple, but also very complex.

You decided what you would look like by selecting your parents. Your parents may be your spiritual parents, or they may not. Isn't it strange that in some cases families fall apart and don't talk for years? Sometimes there is a conflict in personalities and parents or siblings come to detest each other. Other families experience pure love, respect and adoration. Which ones do you think were whole families coming back together and which ones selected each other? Take time to look at the families you know and decide.

Freedom of choice

You decided to suffer on this earthly plane. Whether it is an illness, pain or grief, this is a fixed status that you decided you would have.

The people you meet who mean something along the way are also a fixed status. There are many aspects of our lives that are planned. They have to be, otherwise life would be chaotic. But we also have freedom of choice, freedom to mould certain aspects in any way we want.

Imagine that as part of your plan you have selected to stand on platform 2 of a train station. There are eight platforms, but you have pre-selected platform 2. You stand at platform 2, but then you have a choice of whether to go north or south. You choose south and get on the train. You can choose what seat to sit in and which direction to face. You now have the choice of where to get off the train, either at your final destination or maybe somewhere else along the way. You opt to get off at the next station. Once you do, again you have eight platforms to choose from, all going in different directions and all going to different destinations.

This is a metaphor, of course. But is a simple way of explaining what parts of your life are fixed statuses—that you are on a journey, in this example—and what parts are a blank page, only to be written on by choice—where you go and how you get there.

Whenever I talk of darker matters, never lose sight of the fact that we have asked to be here and that all suffering, whether physical or emotional, has been self-planned and therefore self-imposed.

The best way to explain this is to call on personal experience.

Frank's story

I knew somebody, let's call him Frank, who had suffered from heart and breathing problems for many years. He was suffering from a rare lung disease that could only be passed on genetically.

I watched him suffer. I watched his disease get worse and take a grip of his body and spirit. I could not do anything to ease his pain and anguish, and he died of his disease a short time ago in his mid-forties.

This kind of disease is genetic and was passed on by Frank's father, whom we'll call Tom. Tom suffered from the same disease. His pain and torment manifested themselves in nastiness and he was not nice to his children. He allowed the disease to twist his emotions, to the point of physical hurt to his children and his wife.

Tom's children watched his health gradually deteriorate, but from what I was told they hated him with a passion due to his cruelty.

Tom decided to come back, to suffer this disabling disease, and instead of using his time, like the cancer sufferer I mentioned earlier, to help people, he allowed the disease to distort his perception on life and he subsequently took it out on his family, sometimes cruelly and physically.

Why? Why would he want to leave a wonderful place like the summer lands to be reborn here to suffer disease and hurt his loved ones?

I think the answer lies with his son. Frank saw his father suffer the disease, he also suffered at his hands, only to have the same disease envelop and kill him.

Frank was also made bitter and twisted by the disease. But although at times he was unkind to his children, he was nowhere as cruel as his father was. His experience of watching how badly his own father acted taught him a lesson—he would not want to be remembered in that way. He was cared for by his wife and died with his loved ones around him.

Everybody in this family had decided to come back and live these experiences. The father, the mother, the five siblings, Frank's wife and their children had all planned this revisit for various reasons.

The reasons for us coming back are personal to those who have returned and I don't profess to know all the answers. All I do know is that a life here is a blink of an eye compared to the infinity of real life in the world of spirit.

So if we choose to come back as part of our eternal striving towards perfection, then why do certain people commit horrendous and evil acts? Does evil exist and what part does it play in everything I have been discussing?

Evil

Just because we are of a different form does not automatically change our personality as soon as we pass over. We are different, but our weaknesses are not caused by our physical body, they are caused by our spirit. Being mean and evil in spirit is not a metaphysical issue, as doctors and psychiatrists believe. It manifests itself physically, but an evil spirit is an evil spirit any way you look at it.

If you are bitter it will affect you physically, and if you allow your physical illness to affect you mentally, then you will be on an everlasting treadmill of bitterness and regret, spiralling down into darker levels of thought.

We all have the opportunity and the inherent ability to undertake evil deeds. These start with a single thought, which expresses itself in physical actions.

You have a choice: you can either dwell in your own self-pity and darkness, or step out into the light and enjoy what life has to offer. Evil people do not want the light, they want to commit harm. Unfortunately for all of us, reincarnation is available for everybody.

Avoiding evil

I cannot explain what makes a soul evil and at what point it becomes evil. That will always be a mystery and an enigma.

All I know is that evil souls live in the lowest realm with like-minded people. They are bitter and twisted and will always feel as though they are not at fault for what they have done and that existence has singled them out for purgatory. They are so wrapped up in themselves that they cannot, or do not want to, see the light and realise that everyone of us has the opportunity to progress. So they live in their own nightmares—in their own dark thoughts and deeds.

The lowest realm is very close to earth and they can, if they are able, impose their influence on weak souls. Have you ever heard someone say that the voice in their head told them to do something?

Always stay away from Ouija boards or séances unless they are controlled by experienced mediums. Playing with these toys can open up channels for dark souls to impose their influence on and even control you. Spirits can contact us through mediums, so why can't evil spirits do the same?

On earth, while the evil may manifest itself as mental illness, these monsters have not performed those dreadful acts because they are mentally ill, they are just plain evil. They have no remorse and would do the same again given the chance. This unfortunately is where the system fails. The hierarchy on this planet has to pigeonhole everything without looking at the true reasons behind such actions. So these people are treated with drugs, whereas it is their soul that needs treatment.

Go to hell?

The next question is where these people go when they die.

Let me get one thing clear here: there is no hell, at least not the kind we read about or see at the movies, the devil with horns, fire and brimstone and eternal pain. We judge ourselves, we are never judged.

Let me ask you a few questions:

- How does the parent feel who has lost his or her young child to a paedophile?
- How about a man who has been tortured in some remote country by terrorists?
- How does someone who has been diagnosed with cancer feel, along with their immediate family?
- Or a woman who suffers from severe depression or constant pain?

Although these conditions are self-inflicted and self-imposed, these people would all say that their lives are like hell.

I want you to imagine an onion. This onion is made up of many layers. Our world and the spirit world are also made up of layers. The earth is the core and the spiritual world and its own infinite layers all form part of the same onion.

When you die, you don't catch a train and go on a journey, all you do is stay in the same place and move to a higher level—a different vibration. A good comparison would be an office block. All you have done is get into the metaphorical lift and go to a higher level. It's still called Spirit Plaza; you are in the same place but also somewhere else.

Whether you are an evil spirit or kind and good, everybody has the same right to progression and betterment. But some people are so wrapped up in themselves they just cannot see the bigger picture. They have to feed their hunger for the dark side so intensely that they cannot see the light. So when they die, they blame everybody else and take no responsibility for their own actions. Do you know people like that here on earth?

The Great White Spirit never judges; it is us who judge ourselves. Weak souls blame others for their misgivings and never take any responsibility. If they do not take any responsibility for their actions, then how can they accept their wrongdoing and offer themselves opportunities to improve?

Life deals in dark and light, black and white, pain and pleasure. The negatives cannot be constrained to the earthly plane alone and there is no bad in the summer lands, so these people have got to go somewhere. Evil serves no real purpose in the spirit world, and those energies that are evil are banished to a realm that is dark and grey. They go to the lower realm.

Where did evil come from?

Where did evil come from and why does it continue to prevail?

Let's go back to birth and the premise that two loving, spiritual energies gave birth to a perfect energy, which left the spirit world to start its journey to spiritual enlightenment here on earth, only to be tainted somehow and decide over a period of time that he or she would commit heinous acts against innocent people.

Like spirituality, evil has many levels: from cruelty to animals, to bullying, mental and physical cruelty to others, right up to the extreme of severe violence, inflicting intolerable pain for pleasure and murder.

But where does this dark energy come from?

Evil is there so that better people can learn of it and from it, and do whatever they can to battle it. It is an energy that has been around since the start of time, even before. It is a by-product of eons of life, it is the waste of life, like the toxins our bodies produce that we don't need and cannot use. Evil is a progression of the smallest thing that has grown over many, many millions of our years.

Evil is a choice that we can all make. We can decide to do something evil, or frown on it and those who deal in it. Evil is a necessity. It is the dark whereas spirit is the light. There has to be evil. But we do not need to know where it comes from, we do not need to know why it is there, all we need to know is that we have to continually be on our guard against it and combat it.

The progression of evil

When a child is born on earth, there are no sign that he or she will grow up to be a demon, because that is what such people really are. A baby boy is innocent: he needs 24-hour nursing, he needs to be changed and cleaned regularly. He grows to a toddler and offers immense pleasure to his parents, who in this case are normal people, just like you and me.

When he gets to 6 or 7, he is very shy but he is also very loving, telling his father that he loves him on a regular basis. When he is a little older, say 9 or 10, he starts to show a tendency to be disruptive at school, being disrespectful to his teachers and fighting in class. His parents are called in by the school on a regular basis to discuss their son's behaviour and lack of ability.

The boy turns 11 and starts secondary school. He is now demonstrating behaviour problems, smoking weed, befriending the wrong type of person. He is sometimes excluded from school, has a violent temper and is very spiteful and selfish, only seeing what he can gain from situations.

He drops out of school at the age of 15. He has turned into quite a handful. He shows no respect to his parents. His addiction to marijuana has now got to the stage where he wants and needs it every day, and his parents suspect that he could be trying other types of drugs. Whatever expensive items he had are now gone and he has stolen lots of his parents' and siblings' belongings to sell to buy drugs. He lies and he cannot be trusted.

The police knock at the door and the young man is arrested for torching a car. The parents are devastated. He is let off with a final warning, knowing that next time he will be in court. The parents learn of other misdemeanours after the final warning and are totally confused as to why he would be so stupid. There are signs of him being a member of a gang.

Six months later the son is arrested for being involved in a gang stabbing. The parents have known that he would grab a knife from the kitchen when cornered—and that is against his own family—but they never thought he would kill someone.

I am sure that this brief overview will touch many families who have gone through similar situations. But where did this all start? Was the boy born evil or did evil attach to him at a certain point in his life? His parents think that they must have done something wrong. But they have another son and he is a cherub, a little angel.

I am convinced that a boy like this is a new soul. He is not inherently evil, he just does not like himself and cannot handle the thoughts in his head, so he has decided to take a path that distracts him from these thoughts. Also he is very weak and can easily succumb to the dark energies, who pick on weak spirits to get them to undertake things they cannot understand.

I believe that dark energies can reincarnate, but not in the way normal spiritual energies can. For us to reincarnate we need the help and guidance of highly evolved spiritual energies. The dark energies have evolved to a very low vibration and therefore do not have the ability to come back here, but they are able to reincarnate their thoughts into the weak minded.

If this boy were to accept the way he is and then rid himself of bad thoughts, he would learn to like himself better. He would change his outlook, feel better about himself and become stronger. He would not need the support of criminals and hence look towards the light. I believe that if he did this, the bad deeds would stop and the channel for the dark energies would be closed.

This is called 'turning your life around'. Many gangsters have done this and gone on to help others. So we can deduce that people who are evil can change for the better. Evil has gripped them, but evil can also be banished. It can be compared to a disease that can be treated and subsequently destroyed. The person has been healed, but the disease is still there for others to be infected by it.

But for some people, the fear they impose on others makes them feel important. Some also welcome the dark energies and use them for personal gain and power, sucking in the weaker ones.

There are other people who welcome the disease, as this makes them feel better about themselves. And as they welcome it, it takes hold of them like a cancer, to the point that it changes their lives for ever. They commit horrendous acts, impose suffering on others, are sent to prison on life sentences, then they die in prison with no regrets or remorse. When they pass over there is only one place they will go, and they will stay there until they accept what they have done, feel remorse and are sorry, then look up at the light for help. It is only then that the summer lands are there for them to enjoy and for them to see what life is really about.

As I have said before, the Great White Spirit does not judge; it is us who judge ourselves. Each and every spirit has the divine right to self-improvement and betterment, and this is without any prejudice, no matter who or what you are.

Control and Hierarchy

Here on earth, there will always be governments and there will always be those who are governed. This is a necessary part of life, as there always has to be control, management and the subsequent hierarchy.

This also applies in the spirit world; it has to. However, instead of control measures, these higher levels of existence are inhabited by spirits who have achieved far more progress than we have.

The physical worlds, universes and solar systems are all infinite. This means that there will be races of beings and animals that are much less developed than us, and some much more developed than us.

The most important thing to remember is that all kinds and levels of existence come from spirit energy, and are therefore as one. Nevertheless, differing solar systems will maintain differing kinds and levels of life.

All physical life will have a life span; this could be 3 days for some insects, 70 years or so for humans, or hundreds of years. But when the life form expires, the remaining spiritual energy has to go somewhere. When we die, as I have outlined, we go to the summer lands. Another life form will have a different set of surroundings. That energy may be way up the spiritual food chain or way down. The lower levels of life will progress to our level, whereas we may progress to some other form and so on.

A higher intelligence

That said, where did humans come from? Where do we fit in the hierarchy?

All life on earth has come about through evolution. But a higher level of existence intervened in the general process of evolution and added a very important ingredient, the human genome. This was introduced thousands of years ago by selecting a certain kind of primate that was the ideal candidate for intelligent life, thus enabling us to inhabit the earth.

We need to live here because we need to experience physical life and all of the traumas and hardships that come with it. What makes us different to the animal kingdom is intelligence.

If intelligence was able to evolve at will, then the majority of the animal kingdom would have become far more intelligent than it is now. It is only human beings who have this level of intelligence.

All animal life has been designed to maintain the earth's equilibrium, and the animal kingdom works hand in hand with the earth itself. The earth was created for us. And if that is so, then the earth must have been created by an intelligence far more progressive than ours.

This intelligent life created this planet for us, and created the solar system, the universe and our sun, all in place and working in complete harmony, just to maintain the conditions in which we live. We are from the light and come back here to learn life lessons.

Such an intelligent life is not going to be evil or impose pain on us. It will keep away, allow us to get on with things and learn our own lessons. It is probably working on something similar somewhere else for when this plane expires in the next million years or so, or even developing planets and solar systems for other life forms.

So if there is a higher intelligence that is controlling and managing us, why does it allow turmoil and evil to manifest themselves on earth? We are like children to this intelligence. If you leave a bunch of kids alone in a house, what you get is chaos. That is what we have on this planet.

Nevertheless, there are leaders, energies in high positions, and there are very many of them. I do not believe that there is just one god, but an infinite amount of them, with an infinite number of energies below them and again above them.

I do believe in Jesus. I believe that he presides over the earth within this hierarchy, and that we are all his children.

We all have the freedom, ability and opportunity to become as good as we can—it will simply take infinity to achieve it.

Guardian Angels

Guardian angels have been around for thousands and thousands of years.

Don't believe what you may read about the dark angel falling from heaven and forming an alliance with the devil. It is complete nonsense.

Guardian angels are very real and perform important roles. They are among the most highest of spiritual beings that have attained spiritual progression and are governors of our planet and also the summer lands. They are the guardians of our universe, and in turn of our spiritual realms. However, they are not of the highest order and they still serve the Great White Spirit.

A guardian angel has the ability to change what happens on this earthly plane with a physical and spiritual presence. They have the ability to show themselves as they really are, or if needed to materialise as humans here on earth. It truly is what science fiction movies are all about.

I have read many personal stories about people who have been touched by angels who came to them as a man or woman on earth to save them. Guardian angels have the ability to effect change.

As part of your spiritual progression, I want you to read as much as you can about guardian angels. Buy books and DVDs and investigate them on the internet. You will find these stories fascinating, uplifting and informative.

Spirit Guides

Spirit guides are different from guardian angels.

A spirit guide is a person residing in the spirit world who is there to protect us through thought alone. They are not as progressed as guardian angels and therefore they use thought to communicate with us.

We all have spirit guides, and the number we have depends on what we are here for and what tasks we have to undertake. They are our friends. They are usually not family, as the thoughts from family would be too emotionally involved, which could cloud the common sense they are trying to convey.

Our spirit guides are the little voice in our head where ideas come from, as well as warnings and intuition. They are the link between us and the vast information available in the spirit world.

Your mind tells you when something is right or wrong. This is a natural instinct, and it is helped by thoughts from your guides.

People who may be described as geniuses have a high level of intelligence to compute and use the information they are being fed continuously from their spirit guides. These scientists, leaders in medicine, designers and engineers are pioneers in their field and are here for the greater good.

I want you to get to know your spirit guides and discover who they are and what they do for you. For this you will have to learn to meditate. The next chapter describes a simple method of meditation that everyone can use.

Simple Meditation

Find a room or a place where there is no sound. If you can't do this then buy some ear plugs, but make sure that you can't be disturbed in any way for at least 45-60 minutes. Being awaken from meditation suddenly can be quite a jolt, so it is important to isolate yourself completely from any disruption, as you will need to come down from the meditation in your own time.

Record the time at which you start. Adopt a comfortable sitting position and place your hands on your legs. Make sure that you are completely comfortable, as if you are not this will cause a distraction.

Once you are comfortable and there is no sound, close your eyes and clear your mind, so that all you see is darkness; darken the room if this helps. You may need to practise clearing your mind several times, as it is imperative to allow your mind to deal with only the list of actions you need to perform meditation.

When you have successfully cleared your mind, your eyes are closed and all you can see is darkness, breathe in through your nose and out through your mouth. Concentrate on doing this and controlling your breathing. Breathe deeply and slowly, then exhale slowly so that you have complete control. Again, you may have to practise this several times until you master it. It is a very important part of building the structure of meditation.

After you have cleared your mind and controlled your breathing, think about how you would ideally like to look and the clothes you would like to wear. Insert into your mind the following vision:

It is daytime and all you can see in front of you are the doors to a lift. The doors are made of mirrors and you can see your reflection. See yourself as you really are, or as you would like to look, wearing your choice of clothes.

You to have bare feet and you can feel the ground you are walking on. You are standing on lush, slightly damp, vivid green grass and you can feel it with your toes. (This gives your mental preparations a feeling of reality at the beginning of meditation. With practice you will soon not need this.)

To the right of the doors you see a button with two arrows pointing towards each other. The button is round and metallic, with a thin blue neon light around it. You know before pressing it that it is there to call the lift. Now reach out and press it. The glass doors open slowly and you see your reflection disappear.

You can now see into the lift. It has no mirrors in it, just a gold metallic finish to the back and two side walls. Each of the walls has a silver metallic handrail on it. If you look up, you can see a white suspended ceiling, the kind you have in an office. Everything looks clean and brand new. It has been refurbished just for you.

Walk into the lift. The floor has a deep cream carpet and you feel the sumptuous pile on your feet.

As you turn back towards the lift door, there is a series of buttons on the right. There are 'close door' and 'open door' buttons just like the one outside, then above there are four further buttons in a line going upwards. All look the same with a blue glow around them, but the bottom one says G, then 1, then 2, then 3.

Close the doors to the lift by pressing the 'close door' button. See the doors closing and as they do you see that they are mirrored on the inside. Again, look at your reflection.

Reach out and press button 1. Feel the lift going up slowly. It is a nice feeling. Above the lift doors you see red lights saying G, 1, 2, 3. The light changes from G to 1 and as 1 appears, the lift slowly comes to a stop.

Reach out and press the 'open door' button and the doors slowly open. Step out of the lift.

Sense everything you experience physically and remember everything you see. (It will be different for each person.)

You will know when it is time to leave. When you do, press the button to call the lift. When the doors open, step into the lift and notice its gold walls, silver handrails and cream deep-pile carpet.

Reach out and press the 'door close' button. Watch the doors close and once again see your reflection. Reach out and press G and feel the lift slowly go down. See the red 1 change to the red G on the panel above the doors.

As you feel the lift come to a stop, press the 'door open' button and watch the doors open.

Step out of the lift, concentrate on your breathing and slowly open your eyes.

Stay in the same position for a couple of minutes, concentrate on your breathing and smile, as you have just been in contact with the spirit world and you should feel elated and calm.

Look at the time—you may be pleasantly surprised.

Record in detail what happened in your meditation, either in writing or on tape. If you are sharing experiences with friends and your friend is following this basic technique as well, compare notes.

Carry out this basic technique for several weeks. Remember that floors 2 and 3 are beyond your ability at the beginning. They are where you go to converse with your spirit guide or guides. Only you will know when you can press the button for floor 2.

Your spirit guide will know before you start to meditate. You may be lucky and be given important information during your first meditation. Even if you do not, you will eventually. They cannot wait to talk to you, but it is you who has to make the first move.

It is only through meditation that you can unlock your subconscious, and that will take years of practice to perfect. How deep you are able to meditate will dictate how quickly you get positive results. Practice makes perfect, so meditate as much as you can.

When meditating, do so with the sole purpose of making contact with your spirit guides and concentrate on this aim each time you meditate.

It will be your guides who will take you to the next level, so focus on them only. The best way to start is to ask your spirit guides to show themselves during meditation. Ask to communicate with them and hopefully they will come.

A Time to Remember

My mother was an extraordinary person. I am sure the majority of us say that about our mothers, but really she was very special. She was a fantastic healer and spiritual person, and it was her influence that got me into spiritualism when I was in my mid-twenties.

It wasn't until after she passed that I found out how many people she had helped, with no personal gain to herself. She never took any payment for healing and it was my brother who found her healing book among her possessions after she died. The book was full of names, addresses and telephone numbers and I had been oblivious to all of this.

She already knows how I feel, but the first thing I will do when I pass over is tell her how I feel about her, and say sorry for not being there when she died, and for being a selfish idiot when I was twentysomething. I know what she will do: she will just smile and give me a hug.

When she passed I decided that I would take the lead and arrange the funeral: the coffin, the service and the flowers. All was paid on my credit card and I didn't care what it cost.

I did something else that brought many thanks from my extended family: I arranged a memorial plaque for her. We held another service to lay the plaque with the family. It read:

> She was a mother, a gran. She was a sister and
> aunt—she was an angel. An angel on earth,
> now an angel in heaven.

During the memorial service, as I turned towards my brother, a single white feather appeared, floating from just above head height to the floor. Nobody else saw the feather, only me.

About a year or so later, I was talking to my brother and I mentioned the feather at the memorial service. He nearly choked on his coffee.

He went on to tell me a story. When I was really young my parents had gone to a wedding and my mother had been lent a hat to wear. She hated hats at the best of times, and she got really getting fed up with a white feather on this hat that was causing her distress.

To my brother, that feather was all the proof he needed of an existence after our earthly death.

Contacting the Spirit World through a Medium

I am a big believer in being able to communicate with the spirit world, as long as it is done under controlled conditions.

We all have the ability to communicate, one way or another, with the spirit world, because we are all from the spirit world. It is just that our body makes it difficult, as we think with our conscious mind. Our physical mind is not designed to communicate with the spirit world; it is designed to control our physical body and thoughts.

You may therefore feel the need to consult a medium. A good medium is very hard to find, however. A true medium will not:

- Charge you too much for a reading, if at all.
- Use tarot or angel cards or any crystal balls or gadgets.
- Tell your fortune.

True mediums will use their gifts to form a link with the spirit world through their spirit guides, who in turn form a link with your family and friends.

This is not easy for those in spirit to do and it all has to be put into place first, so don't think that your decision to see a medium was off the cuff. Believe me, it was planned, and in great detail.

There are different kinds of medium:

- Clairvoyant—this is the most common name. Clairvoyants are able to see the spirit in their mind's eye and to have messages passed from their guides and the spirit by thought.
- Clairaudient—the medium is able to hear their guides or the spirit talking to them and can pass on to the recipient what is being said.
- Clairtransient—the medium is able to go into a trance and therefore allows the spirit to take over his or her body to pass on any messages, and/or materialise in some form to offer the message directly to the recipient. The materialisation takes the form of the spirit using ectoplasm, emitted from either the mouth of the medium or the top of the head.

If you have just suffered a loss and you feel that you need to see a medium, I strongly recommend that you contact your local spiritualist church. Speak to the head of the church, who will be only too happy to help. They will arrange a reading for you and may ask for a small donation to the church in return.

Do not—I repeat, do not—waste your time and hard-earned cash on mediums who advertise on the internet, or in newspapers or advertising manuals. You will pay £25-40 for your reading and probably feel deflated and let down. Take my advice and contact the local church.

Most spiritualist churches have open services, usually on a Sunday. You sing a few songs then there is a guest speaker or reader—and you might get a message.

Psychometry

Our physical bodies are made up of flesh, muscle and sinew, bones, blood and genes. When we die, this all dissolves and leaves the bones. If the bones were left to be attacked by the air, they would, in time, turn to dust.

However, our true selves are formed of spiritual energy, an undying, everlasting energy.

During our life on earth we learn to love certain material possessions. It could be a ring, a scarf, a watch, even a painting. It is something we adore, and it is our love that forms a fingerprint of energy on that material object that can be located and found during a psychometry reading.

By holding this object in your hand, a psychometric medium picks up on the energy within the items, which forms a link with the person in the spirit world who could not take it with them.

Imagine a mobile phone number. You have this in your phone and you know it is the link to your friend, so by using the mobile phone you tap in the number, it rings and then you can communicate. It is the same with a cherished object, only the object is the mobile number and the medium is the phone.

Invariably, you will pick up on memories associated with the item as well as general information about the person who owned it. You will not be able to forge a direct communication with the spirit unless you are a trained and accomplished medium.

Auras

An aura is a glow of colour that is emitted from a spiritual mass or being.

If you see pictures of the earth from space, you can see a white aura around the planet. White is the purest of all energies. It is this glow that is the earth's aura being emitted from a pure spiritual source.

You would have thought that all the negative and dark energies that reside on the earth would affect its aura and darken it. However, you can see that the earth remains strong and resolute. Let's not forget that the earth is alive and self-sustaining, and has been so for millions of years. It is going to take a lot more than human beings to change that.

All of us have auras, and these can be seen by a trained medium. Such a medium can offer an aura reading during which they can look into the colours of your aura, and not just read your character but also your physical attributes and ailments, since your physical state has a direct effect on your spirit and vice versa.

Let's investigate what the colours of auras represent.

White—Protection

The different shades of the white aura are:

- **Ivory**—a creamy tone. You are on the up in life, things are looking great and nothing can go wrong. Good luck comes with this shade.
- **Snow**—shiny and sparkly. You are spiritually enlightened. This shade of the white aura can usually be seen at physical death as the spirit prepares to leave the body.
- **Pure**—translucent. You have a very high level of spiritual ability.
- **Smoke**—a sheer, translucent sheet. Change is coming and upheaval will be coming with it.

Gold—Spiritual Leadership

Gold is rarely seen in the human aura. It is a colour of highly evolved spiritual consciousness, often appearing in the auras of holy leaders.

Purple—Spiritual Wisdom, Intuition and Psychic Ability

The different shades of the purple aura are:

- **Violet**—a blue shade. Perfect alignment of a person's mind, body and spirit. True religious gurus have violet in the head area.
- **Orchid**—a light pinkish hue. Spiritual balance and harmony. Found in the auras of people who have reached their own quiet spiritual self-acceptance.
- **Mauve**—a subtle powdery shade. You are humble and always put others ahead of yourself.

- **Lavender**—the same colour as lavender flowers. Budding psychic ability. You have had a spiritual awakening.
- **Grape**—a deep shade, yet lacking shine. You have potential for spiritual advancement, but you need to be making more effort.
- **Plum**—a rich, royal shade. You have found your spiritual path and awoken your intuition. You believe you have already found the 'truth', but in reality your journey is just beginning.
- **Electric**—bright and dynamic. You are totally in the flow of the universe. You are in exactly the right place at the right time.

Blue—Feelings, Emotions and Instincts

The different shades of the blue aura are:

- **Pale**—a sensitive soul, sometimes a little too sensitive. You need to stop putting so much emphasis on the opinions of others.
- **Sky**—strong intuition, though subconscious. You probably have very prophetic dreams, as this is your intuition's way of making you listen.
- **Cobalt**—with your intuition leading you, you can't go wrong. Some people would call you lucky, but in reality you simply act on intuition, which will always pay off for you.
- **Royal**—making all the right decisions in line with your gut instinct, you are now well and truly on the right path. You are comfortable in your own skin and relate honestly with others.

- **Navy**—you enjoy life on the safe and steady side. Never one to rush in, you make decisions slowly after a lot of contemplation.
- **Indigo**—your intuition is highly evolved to the point that you often fascinate people with your psychic ability.

Green—Growth, Healing and Abundance

The different shades of the green aura are:

- **Lime**—outside forces are causing you to act in a way that isn't in tune with your heart's desire. Other people might view you as a liar and a cheat.
- **Spring**—the colour of new shoots in the garden. You have natural healing abilities, a skill that will flourish and benefit the lives of others if you practise and nurture it.
- **Iridescent**—you have an open mind, and this allows the good things in life to flow to you.
- **Emerald**—you are gifted in the healing of trauma. Paramedics, doctors and nurses often have this colour in their auras.
- **Jade**—you like to give to others and expect nothing in return. Because of this quality, people naturally give to you.
- **Olive**—denial of life's natural abundance. You believe that money is a limited commodity and this 'poor thinking' is reflected in every area of your life.
- **Turquoise**—you are driven to improve yourself. Bordering on obsessive, you need to take a deep breath and learn that all good things will come with patience.

Yellow—Optimism, Youth and Dreaming

The different shades of the yellow aura are:

- **Lemon**—you know who you are and where you are going in life. You have a knack for staying out of situations that won't help you achieve your goals.
- **Buttercup**—you are extremely focused on an outcome. Be sure to stop, take a breath and look around every once in a while.
- **Golden**—the colour of inspiration. Whatever idea you have, go for it.
- **Mustard**—this dull colour indicates a deceptive and manipulative streak.
- **Daffodil**—rigid thinking means that you require constant affirmation from other people. You demand everything from compliments to thanks.
- **Straw**—you like to dream, but don't enjoy the practicality of putting your thoughts into action.

Orange—Kindness, Vitality and Communication

The different shades of the orange aura are:

- **Peach**—you always do what is best for others. Teachers, counsellors and parents often display peach in their auras.
- **Tangerine**—you are a very charismatic person. By concentrating on other people, you make them feel special. You are very confident when communicating with other people about what they need.

- **Pumpkin**—your dreams are about to be realised. You have worked for a long time on a project or idea, and you will soon reap the benefits.
- **Terracotta**—this murky colour appears when you have suppressed your emotional energy, which leads to scattered thoughts and the inability to concentrate. As a result you believe you are an under-achiever.

Red—Creativity, Dynamism and Nervousness

The different shades of the red aura are:

- **Rouge**—you are subconsciously seeking change in your life.
- **Tomato**—you are motivated by great passion, which can be seen in two ways. On the negative side, this colour appears when you lose your temper. However, it can signify positivity when you put passion into a project.
- **Rust**—this is a hallmark colour of anyone who is quick-tempered. This might be triggered by a situation that causes you nervousness, which you vent as aggression.
- **Scarlet**—lust and ego. Ever heard of a 'scarlet woman'?
- **Crimson**—you are naturally creative and have just the right depth of vision to remain inspired.
- **Maroon**—you are able to channel your nervous energy in a positive way. Your high level of self-worth means that you feel greatly empowered in your life's direction.

Pink—Love, Lust, Immaturity and Obsession

The different shades of the pink aura are:

- **Light**—small amounts mean love; too much indicates slavery to love.
- **Rose**—you are loyal and committed in love, perhaps bordering on obsessive. In your eyes, the object of your affection can do no wrong.
- **Salmon**—you just love life. You are very content and truly love your life exactly as it is.
- **Coral**—pure animal lust. Often appears in the auras of teenagers as their hormones emerge.
- **Dusty**—immaturity. Too much of this colour can indicate mental issues.

Brown—Practicality, Earthiness and Common Sense

The different shades of the brown aura are:

- **Tawny**—you have summoned up the courage to tackle a new project. You might be feeling nervous, but please don't be. This next step is vital for your growth and will teach you valuable new lessons.
- **Caramel**—you are working on a project with your hands. This project is sensible, and you are taking practical steps to complete it.
- **Khaki**—too much thinking has clouded your mind and judgement. This comes from following your head instead of your heart. Try becoming still and listening to your intuition.
- **Beige**—the fog in your mind is lifting and you are regaining some clarity of thought.

- **Mushroom**—you feel bogged down, as if life isn't moving as quickly as you'd like it to. This means you're missing a lesson in the detail. Look deeper into the situation.
- **Chocolate**—you have an affinity with the earth's natural resources. You have respect for Mother Nature.
- **Chestnut**—you like to concentrate on the job at hand. Your confidence and discipline mean that you are good at teaching your skills to others.
- **Clay**—you are a maverick. It doesn't matter how long the rules have existed, if you see a better way of doing something, you will do it your way.

Grey—Entrapment and Depression

The different shades of the grey aura are:

- **Light**—you have made decisions that you regret. These decisions have led you to the life you are living now, which you don't enjoy. You are the person who got yourself into this situation, so you need to take steps to correct it.
- **Dark**—your life force is being suffocated by the way you are living. This colour is often seen in people who have a severe condition such as chronic depression. If this colour is identified, you need to take urgent action and seek the help of a qualified healthcare professional.

Black—Defensiveness and Repugnance

Black can only exist if there is no white. Think of it as holes in your aura that need to be filled with intense positivity.

People can sometimes unconsciously put negativity in their aura if they feel they need to protect themselves from someone else.

Those who keep destructive secrets allow these to eat up their aura.

Sometimes people who have been subjected to an intense trauma have holes in their energy fields. In cases such as post-traumatic stress disorder, therapy is required to work through coping strategies that will eventually lead to healing.

Spiritual Healing

Spiritual healing is exactly what it says—healing the spirit.

We have looked at how your physical state can have a profound effect on your spirit and vice versa. The aim of spiritual healing is to offer healing to the spirit body. This is done by the spirit world, through your spirit guides, then through the individual giving the healing, using that person as the channel.

The healer is not miraculous. True healers will advise you that it is the powers of the universe who are undertaking the healing, not them.

It is all done through light and spiritual energy. If you refer back to the aura section, you will be able to see that different colours represent differing sections of a person's psyche. The spirit guide and the channel will be able to see your aura, and they will automatically tell from the colours within that aura what needs attention, whether the problems are emotional or physical.

The energy will offer boosts to different parts of the aura, which in turn will offer that boost to the spiritual body. It is the healing of the spiritual body that will be transposed into physical healing.

An individual undergoing healing may need many sessions or just one or two, depending on the severity of the problem.

Fred's story

A man, whom we will call Fred, had been diagnosed with cancer. His condition was terminal and he only had a few months to live. He was given a recommendation to speak to a man I know who runs a healing pool online. This man was given Fred's details, his address and the exact details of his illness.

Fred and his wife had planned and paid for a sailing holiday before he was diagnosed, and it was going to be a second honeymoon. Fred's wife was excited and was looking forward to the trip.

Fred was put into the spiritual healing pool on three separate occasions over a period of a week. He felt stronger after receiving his first session and decided that they would go on holiday regardless. They would enjoy themselves and forget about the disease.

Fred and his wife completed their journey and his wife commented that it was the most beautiful three weeks they had ever spent together. Three months later Fred still looked wonderful, as though he was totally healthy. It had been the best summer they had had in 40 years of marriage.

He was on chemotherapy, but he had not lost a single hair and had a wonderful red colour to his face. The doctors were amazed. One commented that you wouldn't have known he was ill.

Inevitably, and shortly after the summer ended, the cancer took its toll. Fred's daughter was with him when he passed away and it was what happened then that will stay with her for ever.

At the second of passing, Fred's body changed. His hair fell out, his colour turned to grey and his face was ravaged with the look of pain. At that moment his body sunk as though he had instantly lost three stone.

The healing had held back the ravages and results of his cancer. He still had it, and he was on borrowed time, but it was a combination of the healing and Fred's need and desire for his wife to enjoy their holiday that allowed him the strength to enjoy every moment.

That is the most beautiful story regarding spiritual healing I have ever heard.

Dreams

There are two types of dream:

- The kind that is a result of brain activity due to stress or anxiety, or even a late meal.
- The special kind, where you have been in contact with a higher level of existence and your dream is a memory of that encounter.

It is the latter dreams that are much easier to remember once you wake up.

Many lessons can be 'downloaded' into your subconscious during sleep. This may be information that you need for a particular task or an impending challenge. When you are asleep is the best time to send information to you as your physical consciousness is not over-worked; if it was you would never get to sleep.

Stress and worry can lead to sleepless nights, but regular, healthy sleep is paramount for improving your spiritual awareness.

During sleep, you may experience astral travelling. You are two people in one body, your physical self and your spiritual self. As sleep is a form of meditation, in deep, healthy sleep your spirit body is free to explore.

I remember vividly one dream, probably the most profound and rewarding I have ever had.

A dream of forgiveness

As I have said earlier, my mother was a very spiritual woman on this earthly plane, who was also very meek and mild. She never liked confrontation. However, her sister was a Scorpio, very short tempered, always had an opinion and never suffered fools gladly. The only problem for my mother was that her sister was an atheist and a disbeliever in the paranormal, ghosts and eternal life.

I had this dream around seven years after my mother died. I vividly remember walking from a large house onto a white-painted, ornate stone balcony, the sort you see in stately homes. I could see into the garden and there were many, many people there, obviously attending some kind of relaxed and stately garden party.

My mother was standing on the balcony, facing me, but talking to somebody else. I remember being so excited I rushed towards her, saying how much I had missed her and how so glad I was to see her again.

My attention was drawn to the garden. From nowhere, just over the balcony, came my auntie, walking slowly in a complete daze, dumbfounded by what she was witnessing. I called out to her, but it was though I wasn't there. She didn't acknowledge my mother, either; she just looked around with eyes like dinner plates, totally in awe at her surroundings.

My auntie died eight weeks after I had the dream. I am satisfied now that she would have acted in that way when passing over to the spirit world, and I am sure that once they reunited, my mother would have said: 'Told you so!'

Ghosts and Poltergeists

In 2001, I met a woman whom I fell in love with. Our relationship lasted 10 years until we went our separate ways.

It was a wonderful but complicated relationship. She had separated from her husband some eight years before we met, although she decided, mainly for the family and all of their business ties, that they would stay married and she would keep her married name.

After he had met somebody special and it seemed that he too was moving on, we went out as a foursome and had many good times together.

Our friendship allowed my partner to worry about him less and concentrate on our relationship more. All round, it was comfortable and happy, a little quirky in many people's books, but nevertheless manageable.

He was the man I mentioned earlier and referred to as Frank, who was suffering from diabetes and died. Many strange things started to happen after the funeral.

Frank's young grandchildren would be in their beds and be heard talking to someone. When asked who they were talking to, they would reply emphatically: 'Granddad!'

His daughter started to experience noises and bumps in the house and things were moved from their usual place, a classic manifestation of a poltergeist.

His daughter took his death harder than all of them and we started to get concerned for her. She decided to contact a spiritual medium.

During a reading, Frank referred to me personally, singing: 'Who ate all the pies, who ate all the pies, you fat b*****d, you fat b*****d, who ate all the pies?' This was to pass on the message that now he was thinner, whereas previously he had been fatter.

He also said that he did not want to pass to the light yet. He knew more than we did, because his daughter, through her grief and loss, was on the slide and heading towards a breakdown.

Through the medium, he said that while he was on earth he believed in nothing, now he believes in everything.

He stayed around for a while, they all knew he was here and it was not until a short time ago, when his daughter had improved in health, that he went and all was quiet.

I do not need to watch any paranormal television programmes or read any books regarding ghosts, I had all the proof I would ever need right there.

Fate and Destiny

Fate and destiny play a very important part in both our physical and our spiritual progression. However, you need to be aware that fate only forms 10% of our lives, whereas destiny is 100%.

If every second of our lives were pre-planned, then why would we have the need for spirit guides? If we have a soul plan and plan our lives before we get here, surely we would we want to plan a life free of hassle, worry and pain?

But we can't plan everything. We can only plan the main details, such as:

- Who we are.
- Who our birth parents are.
- What part of the world we are born in.
- Under what star sign and on what date we are born.
- Who we will settle with in marriage or partnership.
- Our friends.
- Our children.
- Our type of work.
- Health issues connected with our birth parents.

These are the basic building bricks and form the foundation to our lives here on earth, and hence the foundation for that physical life as it passes into the spirit world.

However, with fate there is also choice. And with choice inevitably there is chance.

Remember the train station metaphor: you can choose what station and platform to stand on, but you are left with a multitude of choices thereafter.

We all have to learn lessons. If every second of every minute of every day were pre-planned, then we would learn nothing.

As physical beings here on earth, we are like children making our way in life. Our spirit guides are there to make suggestions and open up opportunities. It is part of our destiny to act on the choices of life, and it is these choices that help form our destiny—both working hand in hand.

All we need to know is that we are protected, and remember that to err is human.

Time Travel

Many if not most of today's scientists and physicists believe Albert Einstein's theories of relativity. Einstein also discovered the speed of light, the fastest recordable speed in existence, which is 186,000 miles per second, or 11.16 million miles per hour. The speed of light is also measured in light years, how far light would travel in one earth year. So, if light travels at 11.16 million miles per hour, a simple calculation gives us an amazing figure.

There are 365 days in a year and each day consists of 24 hours, totalling 8,760 hours per year. Therefore light travels 11.16 million x 8,760 = 97,761,600,000 miles in a light year.

These are values and numbers that are on the verge of our human perception.

However, where the real amazement starts is allowing our mind to think about travelling at the speed of light and light years.

The Twin Paradox

Einstein came up with an example to show the effects of what is known as 'time dilation'. Think of a pair of twins, Al and Bert, who are 10 years old and live in a highly futuristic universe.

Their parents decide to send Al to summer camp in the Alpha-3 star system, which is 25 light years away. Bert doesn't want to go and stays home on earth, so Al sets out on his own. Wanting him to get there as quickly as possible, his parents pay extra and send him at 99.99% of the speed of light.

The trip to the star and back takes 50 years. What happens when Al returns? His twin brother is now 60 years old, but Al is only 10 and a half. How can this be? Has Al discovered the fountain of youth?

Not at all. Al's trip into space lasted only a half year for him, but on earth 50 years passed. Does this mean that Al can live for ever? No. He may have aged by only half a year in the time it took 50 years to pass on earth, but he also only lived half a year. And since time can slow down but never goes backwards, there's no way he could grow younger.

Atomic clocks

Atomic clocks are extremely accurate clocks that can measure tiny amounts of time: billionths of a second. In 1971, scientists used these clocks to test Einstein's ideas. One atomic clock was set up on the ground, while another was sent around the world on a jet travelling at 600 mph. At the start, both clocks showed exactly the same time.

What happened when the clock that was flown around the world returned to the spot where the other clock was? As Einstein had predicted in a general way, the clocks no longer showed the same time: the clock on the jet was behind by a few billionths of a second. Why such a small difference? Well, 600 mph is fast, but still just the tiniest fraction of the speed of light. To see any significant differences in time, you'd have to be travelling many millions of miles an hour faster.

This indicates that in theory at least, time travel is possible. However, the faster an object travels the more it increases in mass. The larger in mass the object becomes, the greater the power it would need to propel it. There is no engine large enough or powerful enough to move a rocket or ship at the speed of light.

Astronomers have recently discovered an earth-like planet within our solar system that is two and a half times the size of the earth. We could never travel to it, as with the means of transport now available it would take 10,000 years to reach it. But in the future, who knows. Travelling at the speed of light may be a regular occurrence in the next 50 or 100 years.

Part I Summary

To summarise the basics of what we have learnt in Part I about the truth:

- The earth, our universe, our solar system and all solar systems were born from events emanating from spiritual beings far above our present level of knowledge, and far beyond our level of perception and understanding.
- We are spirit, we are born from spirit and we return to spirit when our physical bodies cease to exist. Spirit is Chi.
- All life forms come from spirit or Chi.
- We are all born. We are born in spirit, then immediately our spirit passes from the spirit world into a human body to start the basics of life and learning. Once that first life ceases, the life's lessons are taken with us and we are reunited with our spirit parents.
- At that time, once we learn and recognise the truth of life and the meaning of our life, we have the freedom of choice to return to the earth through reincarnation, to achieve more lessons and a deeper level of learning that can only be attained by living a physical life.
- This reincarnation is planned by us with our loved ones and is called our soul plan.
- All physical and emotional strife is part of our soul plan. Do not blame anybody or any entity for problems or bad health during your life, as you will

soon learn that it was you who planned them all in the first place as part of your learning programme and striving towards spiritual perfection.

- We can choose to stay in the spirit world if we so wish.
- We are born as spiritual energy in the spirit world, and it is this place that is our real home. The spirit world we come from is the summer lands, and we all have opportunities to progress to higher spiritual realms. This is our birthright.
- The spirit world is based on love, understanding, beauty and the balance of all things.
- All levels of life have applicable levels of control and hierarchy.
- The hierarchy of our world, universe and spirit realm consists of the guardian angels, and there are levels of hierarchy above them.
- Spiritual energy and life are eternal. Once you are born in the spirit world, that spark of energy that is you is eternal.
- The Great White Spirit, which is life itself, is good and has no beginning or end.
- Evil and dark energies exist and these have been around since the start of time. The dark side is the opposite of the light side, and will always be there to tempt us and affect the choices we make while in a physical form.
- Evil and dark energies cannot penetrate the spirit world as they exist on a lower vibration of life. But they can penetrate the physical life, since the physical life vibrates and exists on a similar level.
- We all have spirit guides to protect us from dark energies while we live on the physical plane.

- We all have choices; however, certain parts of our lives are fixed. These fixed elements are known as fate. While the majority of our lives are based on freedom of choice, fate represents a very important part of life.

- When our body ceases to exist, we as spirit life leave the body as soon as physical life ceases. There may be something or someone on this earthly plane that keeps us from passing over to the spirit world. On earth we can see or experience this presence as a ghost or poltergeist.

- We are able to communicate with those who have passed over through a medium, who in turn forms a link with his or her guides, who in turn form a link with the energy or person who has passed. This is a link where information can pass freely from the spirit realm to us here on earth.

- We all have psychic ability in some form, and this can be improved or enhanced through meditation, awareness and learning. Stay away from uncontrolled séances and Ouija boards. Use meditation only for finding and connecting with your guides. They will protect you and know what to do.

- As spiritual beings, the aura that is emitted from our spiritual body can be seen clearly by a trained eye. Healing can be given to the spiritual body, which in turn will be transmitted to the physical body. The present state or condition of both the spirit and physical bodies can be gauged by reading the aura.

- Our guides, and in turn our loved ones, can communicate with us though our dreams.

- The earth is a living organism that forms life and sustains life. The animal kingdom works and lives in complete harmony with the earth. The earth needs oxygen-breathing life to survive. The earth itself, through its breathing system (the trees), inhales carbon dioxide and exhales oxygen. All air-breathing animals inhale oxygen and exhale carbon dioxide. Life and earth sustain each other.

- When a cruel, evil and uncaring person's body dies, they will not be able to pass over to the spirit world as their bitterness, hate and self-pity would contaminate it. Therefore they go to the dark realms. There they have no pity on those they have hurt, they feel only pity for themselves and bitterness for how life treated them. They will have the opportunity to lift their head, look up to the higher realms and improve their life. Invariably, this does not happen. All they do in wallow in self-pity and use this negativity to impose their will on the earth.

- When the bodies of peaceful people die, we live on and pass over to the spirit world, a place that is beautiful and full of love, where colours are vibrant and rich and where we are united with our loved ones who have passed over before us.

Learn to be a better person, using the guidance in Part Two. Give love and you will receive love. Care for others and you will live a life of eternal bliss.

Part Two

Be a Better Person

Introduction

In Part One you have had access to the glorious truth. You now know where you come from, generally why you are here, and where you go when your body fails to exist.

You know that there are many gifts available to us all here on the earthly plane and how to use them for the greater good.

You know that you have to meditate to contact your guides and possibly your loved ones, and that in time and with lots of practice there is a whole new world there waiting for you to explore.

You have learnt that we can be used as channels to heal and that we can be read by our auras, those beautiful colours emitted by our spiritual bodies. These auras can unlock what we need to feel healthier and be better people.

You are aware of how significant dreams are and how important it is to record them.

I want you now to move upwards in your outlook on life. I want you to take the lessons you have read—and hopefully will read again and again—and use this information to take you to the next level. This is the level at which you start to improve yourself and become a better person.

The Beginning of Your New Life

I want you to spend some time analysing yourself and listing all of the things about yourself that you don't like. I mean everything!

To enable you to improve your life, you must first identify every single thing, no matter how big or small, that you don't like about yourself.

This list could be bigger than you expected. If it is, don't worry, because now you're a different person than you were a short time ago.

Now you are in possession of some very special information, and that in itself has made you a better person. You are enlightened. As Michael Jackson said, start with the man in the mirror.

You want to be a better person and all good things begin with a thought—the impetus to do something about it.

You are aware that you are a special person who through change can make a difference, and that some people who have passed over, who could do anything with their new lives, have chosen to be your guide and help you.

Categorise the things on your list into two categories, the physical and the spiritual.

The physical could be, for example:

- I am too fat
- I am too thin
- I am too tall
- I am too small
- I have a big nose
- I hate my hips
- I don't like my hair
- I want more money
- I want a better car
- My house is too small

The spiritual could be, for example:

- I want to be a nicer person
- I need to be more patient
- I want to be more sympathetic
- I want to be happier and smile more
- I want to give more to others
- I want to be more friendly to strangers

Once you have your two lists, go through each item again and cross out everything that you know is impossible to attain. When you have done this, you should be left with two achievable plans for self-improvement, one physical and one spiritual.

At this juncture, you know that it may take a very strong will, and indeed a very long time, to achieve all of your physical goals. Before you finalise your lists, again dispose of goals that you know are attainable, but will take too long to achieve and hence you may fail.

Once you have made your finite physical list, fold it neatly into four, making sure that all the creases are crisp and straight, then put it away in a drawer or somewhere safe. Trust me, all will be revealed.

That will leave you with a list of all the things that you, as a person, are not happy with about yourself on a spiritual level.

Don't fold this list, instead print it off at A4 size and laminate it. Stick it on the wall where you can see it, as it is this list that you need to work on first.

Most of the items on the list that you have stored away are likely to be based on self-gratification and egotism. Of course, if you are overweight, you drink too much or you need to stop smoking, these are things that need to be changed. But how can you undertake such drastic changes to your life if you are weak emotionally? You need to be strong willed to diet and lose weight, or to cut down or stop drinking, or to quit smoking.

Loving yourself more and improving yourself as a person will give you the courage and conviction to take action against those physical habits and lifestyles that are hurting you both physically and spiritually.

Heal and improve your spirit, and the rest will follow.

Gaining Spiritual Awareness

You now have this very important list—what are you going to do about it?

Only you can improve yourself, so you have to take action. You need to decrease the negatives and increase the positives.

First, you have to learn how to love yourself again.

You're not a bad person; if you were you wouldn't be reading this book, as you simply wouldn't care enough. You've just walked off the path a little, and we need to get you back on track.

You have the tools, you have the ammunition, and all you need now is to learn how to use them. With practice, practice and practice you will improve your skills beyond your imagination. The skill I'm referring to is meditation.

Meditation is the first, second and last basis for attaining deeper spiritual awareness. This awareness alone will change your outlook on life and enable you to form a firm foundation for self-improvement.

Mind over matter

I was once told a story about a very ambitious salesman. He was selling life insurance, but he wasn't selling all that much.

This was reflected in his bank balance, which in turn translated to what car he could afford to drive, at that time a battered Ford Mondeo. His goal was to own a Mercedes.

One day he decided to join a self-help group, where he was advised to see a self-help guru. During his first session he tried to explain why he thought he was a failure and was not successful. The guru laughed.

'Try this, friend,' said the guru. 'I want you to go to a Mercedes dealer and find the car you want. I want you to sit in it, smell the leather and inspect every inch of the car so you know it inside out. Get the brochure. Then once you've done this, arrange a test drive. By the time you've finished you will have learnt about every inch of that car, how it feels when you drive it and how it sounds. You will remember the noise the door makes when you close it. Allow yourself to be totally absorbed by the car.

'Then, after you have logged in your mind every detail, every night before you go to bed I want you to lay alone on the bed and close your eyes. I want you to imagine that you get in the car. I want you hear the door closing and smell the leather when you sit in the car, how the seat feels around your body. All of the dials, the feel of the steering wheel in your grip, the sound when you press the start button. The feel and sound of the drive.

'I want you to do this each and every night for three months.'

The salesman did exactly what the guru said. He lay alone on his bed every night imagining his drive and living through every second.

One day three months later, after he had showered, had his breakfast and swallowed the final gulp of coffee, he walked to his car to drive to work. He stood there confused, then anger filled his head and he wanted to shout. Somebody had stolen his car. Somebody had come onto his drive during the night, stolen his car and left this rust bucket that obviously was not his.

Somebody had stolen his Mercedes!

After that, his bosses were amazed at how quickly he turned things around. Soon he was salesman of the month. The first thing he did was go to that Mercedes showroom and buy the car that had been taken from him so blatantly that morning.

It was through meditation that this man learnt mind over matter. It was meditation that removed his self-doubt and replaced it with another reality, maybe a dream at the time, but one that soon became real.

The foundation of a better life

Overcoming your inhibitions, self-doubt and lack of self-worth will form the foundation of your better life. You will not be able to eradicate negative thought by yourself, you will need help, and that help is there in the universe waiting for you to find it and ask for it.

It is being aware of what is around you that is important. And what is all around you is the universe, the powers of the universe, and your loved ones in the spirit world. All they want to do is help and make you happier, healthier and more comfortable. The higher your level of intelligence and understanding, the more understandable reality will become, and the more the simpler things in life will prevail.

You need to obtain help from the higher source, the Great White Spirit and the powers of the universe, because if you deserve it you will be granted it. And you do deserve it.

Positive Thoughts

Is your glass half full or half empty?

I am sure you have heard that saying dozens of times. However, I want you to keep on reading it, and hearing it, over and over again.

You see, your glass has always got to be half full. That's the positive, whereas a glass half empty is the negative. From now on your glass will be half full, waiting for you to fill it again.

Your first lesson is to bring some positivity into your life. I have met many, many negative people and they can drain you of energy. They will never achieve their full potential on this planet, as nothing will ever be good enough for them and they will never be good enough for themselves.

Do you remember when I said that all physical ailments stem from the spirit? We choose our ailments in the spirit world as part of our soul plan. Therefore all positives and negatives are controlled by the spirit. They are controlled by you.

You can only change your life by changing your outlook on life.

Your mantra

Making the first real and solid change in your life starts today. Every day, and indeed whenever you need a boost, recite the following words and phrases. Together these are called a mantra.

This will be your mantra from now on. As time passes and you start to open up your eyes, heart and soul, you may design you own, but for the time being use this one.

I call today upon the powers of the universe.

I call today upon my guides and my loved ones who have passed before me.

I ask you for guidance and strength to see through the darkness.

I ask you to give me a torch of wisdom to increase my enlightenment to that glorious truth.

I ask you for protection during my meditations and for my guides willingly to call upon me.

I ask for strength of spirit and the wisdom to recognise it.

I ask for guidance in order for me to be a better person.

I ask you to shower me with eternal, positive light and thoughts.

I ask the powers of the universe for all things that will improve my life.

I ask the powers of the universe to give me the strength of character to be happy and full of positive thoughts—because I deserve it.

Sit in a meditation position and repeat the mantra twice a day, every day.

When you start meditating using the method detailed earlier in this book, saying the mantra before going into meditation will fill your mind with positive thoughts and energies.

By using the positive mantra on a regular basis and by meditation, you will over time feel calmer, more energised and, more importantly, more knowledgeable.

Meditate and recite the mantra as regularly as you can, and be sure to believe in it, as these are words of truth.

Rules for Being Human

1. **You will receive a body.** You may like it or hate it, but it will be yours for the entire period this time around. You have chosen this and once you realise it, the negatives about your body will not be so important.

2. **You will learn lessons.** You are enrolled in a full-time, informal school called life. Each day in this school you will have the opportunity to learn lessons. You may like the lessons or think them irrelevant and stupid. Nevertheless, it is important to relish them.

3. **There are no mistakes, only lessons.** Growth is a process of trial and error and experimentation. 'Failed' experiments are as much a part of the process as those that ultimately 'work'.

4. **A lesson is repeated until it is learnt.** A lesson will be presented to you in various forms until you have learnt it. When you have learnt it you can go on to the next lesson.

5. **Learning lessons does not end.** There is no part of life that does not contain its lessons. If you are alive, there are lessons to be learnt.

6. **'There' is no better than 'here'.** When your 'there' has become a 'here', you will simply obtain another 'there' that will, again, look better than 'here'.

7. **Others are merely mirrors of you.** You cannot love or hate something about another person unless it reflects to you something you love or hate about yourself.

8. **What you make of your life is up to you.** You have all the tools and resources you need; what you do with them is up to you. The choice is yours.

9. **The answers to life's questions lie inside you.** All you need to do is look, listen and trust. Ask the universe for help and for answers to your questions.

Being a Better Person

When seeking self-improvement, the main goal for all of us is to be a better person. We want to treat other people better, and to treat ourselves better too.

You can't be truly nice to someone else if you can't be nice to yourself.

The first thing to forget is all of the negative things you think about yourself physically. Remember the list you made that you put in a drawer?

Get it out of the drawer—and destroy it. Burn it; rip it up into little pieces; flush it down the loo—anything that works for you.

The only list I want you to keep is the one detailing how you, in your own mind, would like to become a better person. You have told yourself what you have to do.

Your starting point is meditation using the simple system I described earlier and the mantra I have already given you.

Take baby steps. Don't condemn yourself if you fail. The bicycle will always be there for you to hop on again and ride.

Regular meditation will calm the spirit, increase your awareness and offer spiritual enlightenment. The mantra will instil worthiness, keep you safe and ask the universe for guidance.

Meditation and mantra—these are the only two words you need to concentrate on for at least the next three months.

Don't read any more at this time. Just meditate, say the mantra and believe, then read on in three months or so.

Being a Better Person (Part 2)

For the last three months you have been honing your skill in meditation and asking the universe for help and guidance while you are doing so.

Your outlook on life should be truly changed:

- You feel more enlightened.
- You feel more aware.
- You have had some amazing experiences while meditating.
- You have received information about your guides.
- Your dreams have become more lucid.
- You have recorded these experiences in writing or on tape.
- You have told all of your friends about your experiences and how happier and brighter life seems.
- Your friends have borrowed this book and have also meditated. You have been swapping experiences and notes with your friends.

If most of these things are true, then you are learning and opening up to the universe. You will now feel that you want to start putting what you have learnt into practice.

I want you to look at the list of self-improvement goals you made and put up on the wall. Start at the top and work through the goals with the help of the headings in the next chapter.

Take a goal at a time and take baby steps towards achieving it.

Let's say for example that your first goal is: I want to be more self-assured and self-confident.

You need to refer to the following section:

Overcoming Adversity

Turning problems into a positive experience.

Personal attributes:

- Firmness in belief
- Self-belief
- Positivity
- Focus
- Self-control
- Truthfulness
- Resourcefulness

Or this may be more relevant:

Goals

Having goals for self-improvement and achievement in life.

Personal attributes:

- Positivity
- Direction
- Self-improvement
- Focus

Only you will be able to tell which sections you need and extract the phrases that apply to your particular goal.

Once you have the lists of personal attributes for achieving your goals, use them. Instil these attributes into your life. Print out the traits on a sheet of A4 paper, laminate it and put it somewhere where you can see the words every day.

Training your mind

You will see that every phrase in the list of personal attributes is positive. By surrounding yourself with positivity, adding this to meditation and your mantra, you are filling your life with positive thoughts.

You are training your mind to think positively. You are causing your physical state to infuse positive thoughts into your spiritual body. As your spiritual body strengthens, so does your physical body and mind—and so on in a self-reinforcing spiral.

Take your time over this. Isolate each goal, master the positive attributes and surround yourself with positivity.

Let negative people pass you by and only associate with the positive.

Love life, love your family and, most of all, love yourself.

Personal Attributes

Attitude

Your attitude to yourself, your life, the world and others. What others see in you when they first meet you.

Positive attributes:

- Showing love
- Smiling
- Respect
- Listening
- Generosity

Authenticity

The positive part of your character that enables people to trust you.

Positive attributes:

- Honesty
- Trustworthiness
- Being real, not fake

Conviction

Having faith in your beliefs and believing in yourself. If you believe in yourself others will also.

Positive attributes:

- Firmness in belief
- Belief in oneself

Courage

Showing courage so that others will be behind you and believe in you. Having courage to lift your spirit.

Positive attributes:

- Self-belief
- Bravery
- Support for others

Discipline

Not allowing external things to control you, so that you have restraint and can impose authority.

Positive attributes:

- Order
- Restraint
- Self-control

Excellence

Striving towards perfection.

Positive attributes:

- Fineness
- Brilliance
- Distinction
- Merit
- Quality

Goals

Having goals for self-improvement and achievement in life.

Positive attributes:

- Positivity
- Direction
- Self-improvement
- Focus

Habits

A focus on positive habits and ensuring that negative habits are diminished or eradicated.

Positive attributes:

- The ability to control bad habits
- The ability to stop bad habits altogether

- Enjoyment of good habits
- Making mantra and meditation a regular habit

Hard Work

Being willing to work hard to reach a set goal.

Positive attributes:

- Self-esteem
- Focusing on results
- Positivity
- Achievement

Humility

Freedom from arrogance.

Positive attributes:

- Humbleness
- Modesty
- Meekness
- Unobtrusiveness

Initiative

Taking the lead in improving yourself and your life.

Positive attributes:

- Planning
- Ingenuity

- Enterprise
- Resourcefulness

Integrity

Being honest and reliable.

Positive attributes:

- Honesty
- Truthfulness
- Honour
- Reliability
- Uprightness

Journeying

Undertaking your own spiritual journey.

Positive attributes:

- Willingness to undertake the voyage
- Seeing across borders
- Adventurousness

Overcoming Adversity

Turning problems into a positive experience.

Positive attributes:

- Firmness in belief
- Self-belief

- Positivity
- Focus
- Self-control
- Truthfulness
- Resourcefulness

Persistence

Striving towards your goals.

Positive attributes:

- Perseverance
- Diligence
- Determination

Perspective

Your outlook and beliefs.

Positive attributes:

- Having a point of view
- Respecting others' point of view
- Perceptiveness
- Maintaining a positive outlook on life

Potential

Exploiting your abilities to the full.

Positive attributes:

- Capability
- Promise
- Ability
- Aptitude

Practice

Being willing to practise, practise, practise.

Positive attributes:

- Ritual
- Preparation
- Exercise
- Training

Priorities

Giving precedence to the important things in achieving your spiritual enlightenment.

Positive attributes:

- Discipline
- Planning

Sacrifice

Getting rid of the bad to receive and accept the good.

Raymond Bottomley

Positive attributes:

- Willingness to surrender
- The ability to let go
- Perseverance

Making Friends

You may be surrounded by loving, loyal and wonderful friends, and if you are then you are blessed.

If you do not have any true friends, there may be a couple of reasons why:

- You are far too shy to meet new people.
- People do not seem to warm to you.

Shyness

Being too shy is a situation that you have put in place yourself to cope with a profound lack of self-assurance and self-esteem.

You need to learn that you are wonderful. You come from a very special life force called spirit, and you have decided as part of your soul plan to be shy and not to mix well and have friends.

This element of your life is very important to address, as if you don't it will come back time and time again.

Meditate and say the mantra. Ask the universe to give you strength of mind. Believe in where you come from and what you are, and that we are all equal in the eyes of the powers if the universe.

Self-belief is much stronger if you have earned it, rather than been given it as a birthright.

Join a group of like-minded people. Take that first step!

Helping people like you

If people don't warm to you, then you'll need to do a bit more work.

Why do you think people don't seem to like you? You may come over as being:

- Arrogant
- Dislikeable
- Self-opinionated
- Exploitative
- Nasty
- Untrustworthy

Rest assured that if you are reading this and you want to make a change, you're not half as bad as you think you are. You have the strength of character to do something about the way you are, which in itself is honourable.

You need to do some real soul searching and speak to those around you. Say to them that you've put yourself on a self-improvement plan and you need some feedback. Ask them to be honest and tell you what it is about you that they don't like.

You have to be strong. Don't see what they say as criticism; try to see it as advice.

List all of the things they tell you and prioritise them according to how important it is for you to change that particular attribute. Print the list out and work through it, as before.

If you improve yourself, meditate and say the mantra, you will, I promise, have a better quality of life.

Finally, always remember the 3 Cs:

- **Call**—never call people names or ridicule them. If you do this once they will never forgive you.
- **Criticise**—never criticise anybody. We all hate being criticised. To criticise is to judge. If you can't say anything good about someone, then say nothing at all.
- **Condemn**—never condemn anybody for their colour, religion, faith, looks or personality. Once condemned is forever forgotten.

Good luck with your journey and reaching your goals.

Future Possibilities

Here are a few messages from the spirit world for you to bear in mind on your journey:

- Do not worry: this world will live for millions of years to come. And do not worry, when it finally expires, we will have prepared another one for you.
- Your world is going through changes, as you are now. Again, do not be afraid. Things will seem to be drastic, with floods, earthquakes and storms. This is not penance, it is change. All will settle soon.
- Expect to see fantastic changes in medicine. There will be a cure for cancer; there will be a cure for malaria. Many new drugs will be found on the earth.
- The future is great. Surgery will be changed beyond recognition in the next 50 years. There will be no need to enter the body where this can add problems in itself. The use of light for surgery will be investigated and will be commonplace in the future.
- Limbs will be replaced by robotic arms as common practice. People who cannot walk naturally will do so by using cybertechnology. This is around now and will be readily available within 15 to 20 years.
- There will be no further big war, although there will be skirmishes. The main concern is terrorist cells obtaining weapons of mass destruction. This is a real threat. The guardian angels will do everything they can to alleviate and reduce this risk.

- There has been a negative aura set against the spirit world due to some psychics being dishonoured or disgraced. Do not worry. There will be more spiritual enlightenment and this is coming soon. This will be in the form of near death experiences. Read the newspapers, watch the television or look on the internet. You will soon see these events occurring. The people who have been chosen will have remarkable stories to tell.

Closing Words

We all have trials and tribulations.

We all suffer heartache, loss and grief.

We all deserve the right to be happy.

We should learn to love our fellow beings and live in harmony.

Life offers us challenges, and it offers us answers.

Be a better person, learn to accept one another, give people the chance to be good.

Always see the best in people, but always be aware and cautious.

Remember that we all come from spirit. Remember that you are wonderful.

Now take all of these lessons, all of these words, and use then for the greater good.

Use them and help someone. Use them and make someone smile.

If you have made a difference to one single person, then your life on this planet has been worthwhile.

May the positive powers of the universe be with you every day of your life—because you deserve it.